Published By Nicholas Thompson

@ Darren Chilson

The Plant Paradox Health & Easy: Fight Disease and

Control Weight Gain

ISBN 978-87-94477-43-7

TABLE OF CONTENTS

Black Bean Bowl

Ingredients:

- 2 avocado (sliced)

- 2-5th cup of salsa

- 2 tsp. of each

- 3 tbsps. of olive oil

- 5 eggs (beaten)

- 2 can of black beans (rinsed)

- Black pepper (ground)

- Salt

Directions:

1. Take a small pan and heat oil in it. Add the eggs and scramble for five minutes.

2. Place the beans in a bowl. Heat the beans in
   the oven for 2 minute.

3. Divide the beans into 3 serving bowls.

4. Top the beans with scrambled eggs, salsa, and
   avocado. Add pepper and salt according to
   taste.

Coconut Blueberry Ricotta Bowl

Ingredients:

- Coconut milk

- Slivered almonds

- Coconut flakes

- 2-5th cup of ricotta cheese

- 2 tbsp. of each

- H2y

- Half cup of blueberries

Directions:

1. Combine coconut milk and ricotta in a medium-sized bowl. Drizzle h2y from the top and add coconut and almonds.

2. Serve with blueberries from the top.

Energy Bars

Ingredients:

- 1 cup of crushed pistachios

- ½ cup of shredded coconut

- 1 teaspoon vanilla extract

- ½ cup of raw dark chocolate chips

- 1 cup of pitted and sliced dates

- ½ cup of cocoa powder

- ½ cup of chia seeds

- ¾ cups of raw oats

Directions:

1. Use a food processor to smoothly blend the dates before adding the walnuts and continuing to blend.

2. Pour the remaining items to pulse together until they are all evenly mixed.

3. Remove and transfer the dough mixture to a small bowl and knead together, forming small, bar-shaped portions, and place on a lined baking tray.

4. Place in the freezer for a minimum of 3 hours or overnight, then remove, slice, and serve.

Peanut Butter And Chocolate Energy Bites

Ingredients:

- 2 teaspoons of chia seeds

- 1 teaspoon of vanilla extract

- 2 tablespoons of cocoa powder

- 1 cup of peanut butter (sugar-free and unsalted)

- 2 tablespoons of raw oats

- 1 teaspoon of maple syrup

Directions:

1. In a mixing dish of medium size, mix the peanut butter with the maple syrup until evenly mixed.

2. Add in the cocoa powder and vanilla extra, mashing until the cocoa is completely coating

the peanut butter mix, then add in the raw oats and chia seeds, using your hands to completely combine the ingredients.

3. Form the dough into balls and add to silic2 molds or an ice cube tray and freeze for 2 hour, then move the refrigerator.

4. These treats can be kept up to 2 week in the refrigerator or a month in the freezer.

5. This recipe makes about 4-5 servings and takes only 5-6 minutes to prepare.

6. For a slight variation, replace the peanut butter with tahini or almond butter. If replacing with thin, adding a teaspoon of raw or toasted sesame seeds is another option.

Maple Granola With Banana Whipped Topping

Ingredients:

- ½ cup maple syrup

- ¾ cup raisins

- Banana Whipped Topping, optional

- For Banana Whipped Topping

- 8 ounces soft or firm regular tofu, drained (sprouted variety is preferred)

- 1 ripe banana

- 2 cups of rolled oats

- ¼ cup of raw sunflower seeds

- ¼ cup of raw pumpkin seeds

- ¼ cup of raw unsweetened shredded dried coconut

- ¼ cup chopped walnuts

- ¼ cup raw or toasted wheat germ

- 1 teaspoon ground cinnamon

- 2 tablespoons maple syrup, plus more as needed

Directions:

1. Line a baking sheet with parchment paper and preheat your oven to 330 degrees F.
2. Combine oats, pumpkin seeds, walnuts, sunflower seeds, cinnamon and wheat germ in a bowl along with maple syrup.
3. Now in your baking sheet, spread the mixture evenly and bake for about 20 minutes.
4. Stir in raisins and bake for another 5 minutes until the oats are golden.

5. Transfer to another baking sheet or tray and let it cool. You can serve it with banana toppings.

Chickpea Flour Scramble

Ingredients:

Chickpea flour batter:

- 1 tablespoon of flaxseed meal

- ½ teaspoon of baking powder

- ¼ teaspoon of salt

- ¼ teaspoon of turmeric

- ¼ teaspoon or less paprika

- ½ cup of chickpea flour or use ½ cup + 1 or 2 tablespoons of more gram flour

- ½ cup of water

- 1 tablespoon of nutritional yeast

- 1/8 teaspoon of Indian Sculpture black salt for the egg flavor

- Generous dash of black pepper

For veggies:

- 1 teaspoon of oil divided

- 1 clove of garlic

- ¼ cup chopped onions

- 2 tablespoons each of asparagus green bell pepper, zucchini or other veggies.

- ½ green chili, chopped

- 2 tablespoons of chopped red bell pepper or tomato

- Cilantro and black pepper for garnish

Directions:

1. Blend all the ingredients under chickpea flour batter and keep aside.

2. You can also use lentil batter from my lentil frittata.

3. Heat ½ teaspoon of oil in a skillet over medium heat. Add onion and garlic and cook for about 3 minutes until translucent.

4. Add veggies, chili and cook for another 2 mins, then add spices and greens.

5. Cover the veggies with the chickpea flour batter and continue cooking while adding olive oil.

6. Since the mixture tends to get doughy, be sure to scrap the bottom.

7. Cook until the edges dry out. This should take about 5 minutes.

8. Turn off the stove and break the food into smaller chunks then season with salt and pepper. You can garnish with cilantro if you like. Serve with toast or tacos.

Apple Pie Smoothie

Ingredients:

- 4 cups of almond milk.

- 4 tbsp chia seeds.

- 2.1 oz rolled oats.

- 1 tsp ground cinnamon.

- 4 scoop vanilla, vegan protein powder.

- 4 apples.

- 17 oz coconut yogurt.

- 1 tsp ground nutmeg.

- 1 tsp stevia (optional) if your protein powder is rather sweetened you will not require this.

Directions:

1. Portion the dry active ingredients into a bag
    or container for each early morning. Reserve
    your apples so nobody gets to them before
    you do!

2. When it is breakfast time roughly chop the
    apple, discard the core. Add it to the blender
    with the almond milk, coconut yogurt and the
    prepped container of dry components.

3. Blend until smooth and delightful!

Spicy Peanut Butter Tempeh & Rice

Ingredients:

- 22 oz tempeh, cut into 1-inch cubes.

- 6.5 oz wild rice, raw.

- Coconut oil spray.

Sauce:

- 2 tbsp red chili sauce.

- 2 tsp rice vinegar.

- 2 tbsp ginger.

- 3 cloves of garlic (or garlic paste).

- 4 tbsp peanut butter.

- 4 tbsp soy Sauce (low sodium).

- 4 tbsp coconut sugar.

- 6 tbsp water.

Cabbage:

- 5 oz purple cabbage, shaved/finely sliced.

- 1 lime, juice only.

- 2 tsp agave/apple bee-free honey.

- 3 tsp sesame oil.

Garnish:

- Green onion, chopped.

Directions:

1. Mix all of the ingredients for the spicy peanut sauce.
2. Cut the tempeh into 1-inch (2.5 cm) cubes.
3. Add sauce to the tempeh, stir, cover and marinade in the fridge for 2-3 hours or, preferably, overnight. Tempeh is actually

good at soaking up the tastes of the marinade.

4. Preheat the oven to 375° F/190° C cook the rice as per packet directions.

5. Location the tempeh on a nonstick flat pan, spray with some coconut oil, bake in the oven for 25-30 minutes. Conserve any leftover marinade for serving.

6. Mix all of the components for the cabbage in a bowl and set aside to let it marinate.

7. Serve it up: To a bowl or meal preparation container, include tempeh, rice and cabbage. Scoop a little additional of the Tempeh marinade on the top as a sauce. Garnish with green onion.

<h1 style="text-align:center">Vegan Fry-Up</h1>

Ingredients:

For Your hash browns

- 2 tsp walnut syrup

- 1 teaspoon soy sauce

- 1/4 tsp smoked paprika

- 1 large Portobello mushroom, sliced

- 1 big potato, unpeeled

- 1 1/2 tablespoon peanut butter

- For the berries and mushrooms

- 14 cherry tomatoes

- jojoba oil

For Your scrambled tofu

- 1 tsp garlic, crushed

- 4 vegan sausages (we utilized Dee's leek & pumpkin)

- 1 x 200g can baked beans

- 349g pack silken tofu

- 2 tablespoon nutritional supplement

- 1/2 tsp turmeric

Directions:

1. Cook the curry entire in a big bowl of water, then simmers for 10 mins then drain and let it cool. Peel the skin off then coarsely grate.

2. Mix using all the peanut butter and season well. Set aside in the refrigerator until needed.

3. Heat oven to 200C/180C fan/gas 6. Set the cherry tomatoes on a baking dish, drizzle with 2 tsp sunflower oil, season and bake for 30

mins or until the skins have blistered and
begun to char.

4. the beans and simmer following the
   Directions: on the package so that they're
   prepared to function in precisely the exact
   same period as the scrambled tofu.

5. Meanwhile, combine the maple syrup, soy
   sauce, and 1/4 tsp smoked paprika together in
   a huge bowl, then add the chopped
   mushroom and toss to coat from the mix.

6. Leave to stand as you pour 3 tsp sunflower oil
   to some non-stick skillet and bring this up into
   medium heat.

7. Fry the mushroom till just beginning to turn
   gold but not charred. Twist onto a plate and
   keep warm before serving.

8. Place 1 tablespoon oil to the skillet and then
   add spoonfuls of the potato mixture -- you
   ought to have about 4. Fry for 3-4 mins every
   side then squirt on kitchen paper.

9. Crumble the tofu to your skillet and then scatter on the remaining ingredients along with a fantastic pinch of pepper and Salt . If the pan seems a bit dry, add a dab more oil.

10. Fry for 3-4 mins or until the tofu is broken up into bits, nicely coated in the seasoning and warm through.

11. Split everything between 3 plates and serve with a hot cup of tea produced with soy milk.

Coconut & Banana Sandwiches

Ingredients:

- 400ml may coconut milk, shaken well

- vegetable oil, for frying

- 1-2 bananas, thinly sliced

- 150g plain flour

- 2 tsp coconut powder

- 3 tablespoons golden caster sugar

- 2 passion fruits, flesh scooped out

Directions:

1. Sift the flour and baking powder into a bowl
   and stir in 2 tablespoons of the sugar and a
   pinch of Salt .

2. Pour the coconut milk into a bowl, then whisk to combine in any Fat that's split, then step out 300ml to a jug.

3. Stir the milk gradually into the flour mixture to make a smooth batter, then or whizz everything in a blender.

4. Heating A shallow skillet or flat griddle and brush it with oil. Use 3 tbsp of batter to create each pancake, skillet at a time -- some more will make it tricky to flip them.

5. Push 4-5 parts of banana to each pancake and cook until bubbles begin to pop the surface, and the edges appear dry.

6. They'll be a bit more fragile than egg-based pancakes, therefore turn them over carefully and cook other areas for 1 minute. Duplicate to create 8-10 pancakes.

7. Meanwhile, Place the rest of the coconut milk and sugar in a small pan. Add a pinch of Salt

and simmer until the mixture thickens to the consistency of single cream.

8. Use this as a sauce for those sausages and spoon over some of the flame seeds.

Chili Soup

Ingredients:

- 24 ounces can crush tomatoes

- ½ teaspoon olive oil

- 1 teaspoon sea salt

- ½ pound ground beef

- , medium onion, roughly chopped

- C spoon ground canned pepper

- Water cup water

- ½ cup dairy cherry tomatoes

- 1 clove of garlic, crushed

- 1 teaspoon onion powder

- 1 tbsp chili powder

- Oon spoon garlic powder

- Powder tbsp cumin powder

Directions:

1. Fry onion, garlic and ground beef in a pan over medium heat.
2. Then, add fresh tomatoes, can tomatoes, and other spices. Leave to boil over medium to low heat for 15-20 minutes.

Clear Onion Japanese Soup

Ingredients:

- 1 carrot, diced

- 1 celery stalk, diced

- 1 handful chopped crust,

- 1 fist button mushroom, finely chopped

- 1 clove of garlic, minced

- 4 cups water or vegetable broth

- 1 medium sized onion, diced

- Soy sauce to taste

- salt and pepper to taste

- Srirakha to taste.

Directions:

1. Over a medium heat, add some oil and fry the onion in a medium size pot and fry until slightly brown.

2. Then, add garlic, celery, carrots, and vegetable broth or water. Bring to a boil, then simmer for 15-20 minutes.

3. Season with salt, pepper and other seasonings to taste. Wash vegetables with water or broth, then add scallions and mushrooms before serving.

Orange And Cranberry Muffins

Ingredients:

- Olive oil or coconut oil, ¼ cup (extra virgin olive oil or coconut oil is recommended)

- Monk fruit or stevia, ¼ cup

- 3 large eggs

- Orange zest, 1 tablespoon

- Baking soda, ¼ teaspoon

- Coconut flour, ¼ cups

- Sea salt, ½ teaspoon

- Dried cranberries, unsweetened, ½ cup

Directions:

1. This is an easy recipe to assemble and bake within a short period. To begin, line and

lightly grease a muffin tray with either paper or silic2 cups.

2. Add the baking soda, sea salt, and coconut flour together to be blended well using a food processor. Preheat the oven to a temperature of 350 degrees.

3. In the food processor, add in the eggs, sweetener, and orange zest and continue to pulse the ingredients together until well mixed.

4. Remove the mixture and transfer into a large bowl, then fold in the dried cranberries with a fork or by hand.

5. Using a spoon, scoop the muffin batter into each of the muffin cups, filling cups ½ to a max of 2/3, once cups are filled place in the oven for approximately 18-20 min.

6. Remove the tray to cool slightly, for 5-6 minutes, then gently remove the muffins place on a wire rack to cool. It's safe to keep

muffins (sealed) at room temp for three days

or the refrigerator for up to 2 week.

Walnut Bread

Ingredients:

- Chia seeds, 1 tablespoon (You can substitute flax seeds if desired)

- Sea salt, ½ teaspoon

- Caraway seeds or a similar seed or herb, 1 tablespoon

- Walnut butter, ¾ cups

- Almond flour, 1/3 cups

- 4 eggs, lightly whisked or beaten

- Baking powder, 1 teaspoon

- Monk fruit or stevia, or a similar low carb sweetener, 1 tablespoon

Directions:

1. To prepare for the bread, preheat the oven to a temperature of 350 degrees.

2. Add parchment paper or a silic2 mat, and a light sprinkling of butter or grease to a loaf pan (9 x 5 inches).

3. If a silic2 tray or pan is used, no mat or parchment paper is needed.

4. Walnut butter can be made from scratch if it is not available in a local store or supermarket.

5. To create walnut butter, add 2 cup of walnuts to 3 cups of water, and allow them to sit for about 2 hour to soften, then drain and pour into a food processor or blender.

6. Pulse the walnuts until they are smooth. In some cases, you may not need to soak the walnuts to create a creamy texture, which is the desired result. The blending process shouldn't take more than 5 minutes in total.

7. Transfer the walnut batter to a large mixing bowl and add in the rest of the ingredients, then place mixture in a loaf pan and in the oven for45-50 minutes or until well d2.

8. The center of the loaf should be clean when using a toothpick to test. Let the loaf cool completely. A flat surface is also a good option for cooling the loaf before slicing to serve.

9. Walnut bread keeps well at room temperature in a sealed container or wrapped in plastic for up to 3 days. It can also be refrigerated for up to 2 week or longer.

Green Smoothie

Ingredients:

For every cup of water:

- ½ mint branch with its stem

- ½ avocado

- 3 to 6 drops of stevia

- 1/2 cup of ice

- 1 cup of romaine lettuce

- ½ cup of baby spinach

- 4 tablespoons of lemon juice

Directions:

1. Put all the ingredients in a blender and put it on high speed until it's all smooth.

2. Add more ice if it's too liquid or more water if
   it's too thick.

Avocado Salad And Cilantro-Pesto Chicken

Ingredients:

Chicken

- 1 tablespoon avocado oil

- 4 ounces of skinless, b2less chicken breast, cut into equal strips

- 1/4 teaspoon of iodized sea salt

- 1 tablespoon of lemon juice

Pesto

- 2 tablespoons of lemon juice

- 1/2 diced avocado

- 2 tablespoons extra-virgin olive oil

- 2 tablespoons of lemon juice

- 1/4 teaspoon iodized sea salt

- 2 cups of chopped cilantro

- 1/4 cup of extra-virgin olive oil

- Sea salt to taste

- 1 1/2 cups chopped romaine lettuce

Directions:

1. Heat the avocado oil in a small pan on high heat.
2. Place the chicken strips in the pan and pour the lemon juice and salt.
3. Fry the chicken strips for 2 minutes; turn them and fry for another 2 minutes, until they're completely cooked.
4. Remove and save.
5. For the Pesto, all you need to do is put the ingredients in a mixer and blend them until they are all smooth.

6. For the dressing, put 1 tablespoon of lemon juice over the avocado, and the bind the other lemon juice tablespoon with the olive oil and salt in a jar and shake until is homogeneous.

Italian Healthy Breakfast

Ingredients:

- ¼ teaspoon red pepper flakes, crushed

- 10 cups fresh baby spinach, chopped

- 1/3 cup scallion, chopped

- 2 tablespoons olive oil

- 1 tablespoon fresh parsley, chopped

- 4 organic eggs

- Salt and pepper to taste

Directions:

1. Preheat your oven to 400°Fahrenheit.
2. Heat over medium-heat in a pan and cook the scallion for about 5 minutes.

3. Add the red pepper flakes, spinach, and black pepper, and stir for about 5 minutes.

4. Move the spinach mixture, removing excess liquid.

5. Make 4 wells in the spinach mixture.

6. Carefully, break an egg in each well.

7. Bake in oven for 15 minutes or until the egg whites are set.

8. Top with parsley and serve.

Tasty Breakfast Hash

Ingredients:

- 1 ½ lbs. grass-fed b2less chicken breasts, cubed

- 2 tablespoons olive oil, divided

- 1 tablespoon thyme, fresh chopped

- 2 tablespoons fresh lime juice

- 1 cup scallion, chopped

- 1 cup homemade chicken broth

- 1 tablespoon oregano, fresh chopped

- 4 garlic cloves, minced

- 1 medium white onion, chopped

- 2 celery sticks, chopped

- Salt and black pepper to taste

- 2 large sweet potatoes, cubed, peeled

Directions:

1. Add 1 tablespoon of oil into pan over medium heat and cook the chicken sprinkle with salt and pepper for about 5-minutes.
2. Transfer the chicken to a bowl.
3. With the same pan heat remaining oil over medium heat and sauté celery and onion for about 4 minutes.
4. Add in the garlic and herbs and sauté for about 1 minute.
5. Add the sweet potato and cook for 10 minutes.
6. Add the chicken broth and cook for an additional 10 minutes.
7. Add in the cooked chicken and scallion and cook for 5 minutes.
8. Stir in the lime juice, salt and serve.

Chickpea And Apple Pesto Pasta

Ingredients:

- 2/3 cup chickpeas ready cooked and rinsed

- 1/3 cup basil pesto

- ¼ cup apple, cored and cubed

- 2 tablespoons of lime juice

- 3 cups of cooked whole wheat pasta or non-wheat pasta if preferred (Rigatoni or Fusilli are good choices)

- 2 packed cups of arugula (rocket) or spinach

Directions:

1. Cook the pasta by following the Directions:given by the manufacturer. Drain and rinse thoroughly.

2. Put the apple, chickpeas and lime into a bowl and mix together until combined.

3. Add the pasta and pesto to the bowl and toss it together.

4. Finally, add the greens and gently combine it into the rest of the ingredients.

5. The bowl can be brought to the table for people to help themselves, or you can plate it up into individual bowls.

6. Add freshly ground black pepper and freshly squeezed lime to taste.

Spicy Vegetable Noodle Soup

Ingredients:

- 1 teaspoon of chili sauce or sriracha (add more to taste if you like it hot).

- 1 cup (packed) Bok choy, kale or dark leafed cabbage.

- 1/3 cup mushrooms, sliced.

- ¼ cup green onion, sliced.

- 3 cloves of fresh garlic minced or grated.

- ½ thumb size piece of fresh ginger, peeled and grated.

- 4 ounces of Udon (or other variety) noodles (cooked according to Directions:on the packet).

- 3 cups of vegetable broth (preferably homemade. If shop bought choose low or no sodium varieties).

- 1 lime cut into quarters.

Directions:

1. While the noodles are cooking bring the vegetable broth and chili sauce to the boil on the stove and then turn down to simmer.
2. Add the mushrooms, onion and garlic to the broth and after 1 minute add the greens and simmer for a further 2 to 3 minutes until the greens have wilted.
3. Add the cooked noodles to the broth and vegetable mixture and combine through.
4. Serve in bowls and eat immediately while hot.

Middle Eastern Couscous Bowl:

Ingredients:

- ¼ cup sliced red onion

- ¼ cup chopped fresh parsley 2 tablespoons lemon juice

- 2 tablespoons extra-virgin olive oil

- Optional: crumbled feta cheese or vegan cheese for topping

- 1 cup cooked couscous

- ½ cup chickpeas, rinsed and drained

- ½ cup diced cucumber

- ½ cup diced tomatoes

Directions:

1. In a bowl, combine the cooked couscous, chickpeas, cucumber, tomatoes, red onion, and fresh parsley.

2. In a separate small bowl, whisk together lemon j uice and

3. olive oil to create the dressing.

4. Pour the dressing over the couscous mixture and toss until well combined.

5. If desired, sprinkle crumbled feta cheese or vegan cheese on top.

6. Enjoy this Middle Eastern -inspired grain bowl that is both refreshing and flavorful.

Harvest Bowl

51

Ingredients:

- ½ cup steamed broccoli florets

- ¼ cup dried cranberries

- ¼ cup toasted pumpkin seeds or pecans

- 1 cup cooked quinoa or farro

- ½ cup roasted sweet potatoes, diced ½ cup roasted Brussels sprouts, halved

- Balsamic vinaigrette for dressing

Directions:

1. In a bowl, combine the cooked quinoa or farro, roasted sweet potatoes, roasted Brussels sprouts, steamed broccoli florets,

dried cranberries, and toasted pumpkin seeds or pecans.

2. Drizzle with balsamic vinaigrette or your favori te dressing and toss until well coated.

3. Serve this harvest bowl as a warm or chilled option, packed with the flavors and colors of autumn.

Root Vegetable Lasagna

Ingredients:

- 1 cup diced celery root

- 1 cup diced rutabaga or turnips

- 1 sprig rosemary, leaves minced

- 2 garlic cloves, stripped and minced

- 1 tsp. iodized ocean salt

- 1/2 tsp. dark pepper

- 1/2 cup water

- 1/2 cup coconut milk

- 2 cups goat's or sheep's milk ricotta or 3 cups coconut yogurt

- 1/2 tsp. dried oregano

- 1/4 cup olive oil, in addition to additional for heating dish

- 1 yellow onion, diced

- 1 cup diced parsnips

- 1 lemon, zested and squeezed

- 1 cup inexactly stuffed basil, julienned

- 2 omega-3 or fed eggs or VeganEggs

- 1 enormous sweet potato, daintily cut (as lasagna noodles; utilizing a mandoline makes a difference)

- 1/2 cup ground Parmigiano-Reggiano

Directions:

1. Preheat the broiler to 375°. Splash a 9 × 13-inch preparing dish with oil, and put in a safe spot.

2. To start with, make your sauce: Heat olive oil in a huge pot over medium-high warmth. Include the onion, and cook 2 to 3 minutes, until translucent. Include the parsnips, celery root and rutabaga or turnips, just as rosemary and garlic, and cook for 15 to 20 minutes, mixing much of the time, until vegetables are delicate. Include the salt and pepper and mix utilizing a submersion blender (or move to a blender), and procedure until smooth. Sauce ought to be consistency of thick tomato sauce. If excessively thick, include water, a little at once. Speed in coconut drain and put in a safe spot.

3. In an enormous bowl, consolidate the ricotta or coconut yogurt, oregano, lemon get-up-and-go and squeeze, basil and the eggs. Put in a safe spot.

4. Spoon a large portion of a cup of the root veggie sauce into the base of your preparing

dish, and layer on 2 layer of the slim cut sweet potato "noodles." Top with a large portion of a cup of the ricotta blend, then rehash until container is full. (It will take three or 5 layers.) Sprinkle the highest point of the lasagna with the Parmigiano-Reggiano, and spread the container with foil.

5. Heat for 35 to 40 minutes, then evacuate thwart and prepare for an extra 15 minutes, until cheddar is brilliant darker. Expel from warmth and let rest 10 minutes before serving.

Tops And Bottoms Celery Soup

Ingredients:

- 1/4 cup minced dried onion or 1/2 red onion, cleaved

- 1 tablespoon cleaved new rosemary leaves, or 1 teaspoon dried rosemary

- 1/2 teaspoon ocean salt, ideally iodized

- 1/2 teaspoon split dark pepper

- 3 cups natural vegetable stock

- 1/2 lemon

- 3 tablespoons extra-virgin olive oil, or avocado or perilla oil, in addition to additional for embellish [optional]

- 2 1-pound celery root, stripped and cut into 1-inch 3D shapes

- 2 celery stalks with leaves, cut into 1-inch pieces

- 3 tablespoons cleaved level leaf parsley, for embellish

Directions:

1. In a huge dutch broiler or substantial pot, heat the 3 tablespoons of olive oil over medium warmth. Include the slashed celery root, celery, onion, rosemary, salt, and pepper, and cook for around 5 minutes, until the celery root and celery begin to soften and darker a piece.

2. Include the soup and lemon, and heat to the point of boiling. Lessen the warmth, spread, and stew for 30 minutes. Mix sporadically and verify when the celery root is delicate. When it is, expel from heat.

3. Move about portion of the blend to a fast
    blender and mix on the purée or soup setting
    until smooth and velvety.

4. Rehash with the remainder of the blend and
    afterward warm the entire clump in the dutch
    broiler for around 5 minutes.

5. To serve, fill serving bowls and enhancement
    with parsley. Shower 1 tablespoon olive oil
    over each bowl, if wanted.

Broccoli Quiche

Ingredients:

- 3 cups of broccoli (chopped)

- 2 and a half cup of mozzarella cheese (shredded)

- 5 eggs (beaten)

- 3 and a half cup of milk

- Half tsp. of black pepper

- 2 tbsp. of butter (melted)

- 2 pie crust (unbaked)

- Three tbsps. of butter

- 2 onion (minced)

- 2 tsp. of each

- Garlic (minced)

- Salt

Directions:

1. Start by preheating your oven at 175 degrees Celsius. Use pie crust for lining a deep pie pan.
2. Take a large saucepan and add butter to it. Add broccoli, onion, and garlic. Cook the veggies slowly until tender. Add the cooked veggies to the pie crust and add cheese from the top.
3. Mix milk and eggs in a bowl; add pepper and salt for seasoning. Add the remaining butter to the milk mixture. Pour the mixture over the mixture of vegetables.
4. Bake the quiche in the oven for forty minutes or until the center has properly set

Tomato Bagel Sandwich

Ingredients:

- 2 large tomato (sliced thinly)

- Pepper and salt (to season)

- 2 bagel (split, toasted)

- 3 tbsps. of cream cheese

- 5 basil leaves

Directions:

1. Spread the cream cheese on the halves of the bagel.
2. Top the cheese layer with slices of tomato. Add pepper and salt for seasoning.
3. Serve with basil leaves from the top.

Pistachio And Cardamom Treats

Ingredients:

- ½ teaspoons crushed cardamom pods or powder

- 1 teaspoon of maple syrup

- 3 tablespoons of coconut oil, melted at room temperature

- 2-3 tablespoons of crushed pistachios

Directions:

1. Blend the entire ingredients together into a small bowl and pour into silic2 molds or an ice cube tray. Freeze for at least 3 hours before servings.

2. Keep frozen until ready to serve. This recipe makes enough for 4-5.

Lemon-Lime Cheesecake Cupcake Fat Bombs

Ingredients:

- 2 teaspoons of lemon juice

- 2 teaspoons of lime juice

- 1 teaspoon of low carb sweetener

- ½ cup of vegan cream cheese

Directions:

1. Mix all ingredients in a small mixing dish and pour into silic2 molds or an ice cube tray.
2. Freeze for 3 hours and serve. Makes enough for 4-5 servings.

Peanut Butter And Jam Porridge

Ingredients:

Peanut butter granola:

- Raspberry chia jam

- ¼ cup raspberries

- 1 tablespoon chia seeds

- ½ cup of rolled oats or an assortment of cereals/nuts/seeds in your pantry

- 1 tablespoon peanut butter

- 1 teaspoon of rice malt syrup

Porridge

- 1 banana, mashed (optional)

- Other toppings

- 2 tablespoon of peanut butter

- ⅔ Cup of rolled oats

- 1½ cup of coconut milk

- 2 tablespoon of peanut butter (optional)

- Whatever you desire! (Such as cacao nibs, coconut syrup, coconut and frozen berries)

Directions:

1. Preheat oven to 360°F.
2. Combine granola ingredients in a baking sheet and bake for about 10 minutes (or until golden brown)
3. Mash raspberries and mix in chia seeds then set it aside.
4. Combine all porridge ingredients in a saucepan and bring to boil.
5. Stir occasionally to maintain its smoothness.

6. Separate the porridge into 2 bowls and add
   granola, chia seeds, and peanut butter as
   desired.

Banana Almond Granola

Ingredients:

- 2 ripe bananas, peeled and chopped

- 1 teaspoon almond extract

- 1 teaspoon salt

- 8 cups rolled oats

- 2 cups pitted and chopped dates

- 1 cup slivered almonds, toasted (optional)

Directions:

1. Preheat the oven to 275°F.
2. Line a baking sheet with parchment paper.
3. Cook dates covered with water in a saucepan over medium heat for about 10 minutes. Make sure the dates do not stick on the pan.

4. Take the mixture off heat and in a blender, combine it with almond extract, bananas and salt until creamy.

5. Add oats to the date mixture and spread out on the baking sheet.

6. Bake for about 45 minutes – occasionally stirring.

7. Remove from oven and let it cool. Enjoy.

Miso Ramen

Ingredients:

- 250 g soba noodles.

- 16 ears baby corn.

- 1 tbsp vegetable oil.

- 8 child pak choi.

- 200 g ready-to-eat beansprouts.

- 2 red chilies, finely sliced on an angle.

- 2 spring onions, carefully sliced on an angle.

- 4 tbsp crispy seaweed.

- 5 tbsp miso paste.

- 2 tbsp soy sauce.

- 2 1/2 cm piece of ginger, grated.

- 12 shiitake mushrooms.

- 225 g smoked tofu, cut into 4 pieces.

- 2 tbsp liquid amino or tamari.

- 2 tbsp black sesame seeds.

- 1 tbsp sesame oil, to finish.

Directions:

1. Put the miso, 1.5 liters water, soy sauce, ginger and shiitake in a large pan. Stir to blend in the miso, then bring to a very gentle simmer. Keep simmering for 5 minutes.

2. Meanwhile, position the smoked tofu in a shallow bowl and pour over the liquid amino. Turn the tofu pieces over to make sure they are soaked well on both sides.

3. Bring a pan of salted water to the boil. Add the soba noodles, bring back to the boil and cook till just tender, about 5 mins.

4. Add the child corn to the miso broth and cook for a further 4 minutes.

5. Heat the oil in a non-stick frying pan over high heat. Gently place the tofu in the frying pan and cook for 2-3 minutes on each side till browned.

6. As soon as the noodles are cooked, drain them in a colander and rinse under cold water, then divide in between 4 serving bowls. Include the pak choi to the miso broth and get rid of from the heat.

7. Divide the pak choi, infant corn and beansprouts in between the bowls - ladle over the miso broth and include the tofu. Garnish with the chillies, spring onions and crispy seaweed. Sprinkle with sesame seeds, drizzle over the sesame oil and serve straight away.

Bali Bowl With Tempeh, Peanuts And Tomato Sambal

Ingredients:

For the tomato sambal:

- 2-5 red chillies, seeds eliminated.

- 2 kaffir lime leaves, finely sliced.

- 1/2 tsp palm sugar, or soft brown sugar.

- 1/2 tsp salt.

- 3 tomatoes.

- 2 shallots, or small red onions.

- 4 cloves garlic.

For the tempeh:

- 125 g tempeh, sliced up or fallen apart into little pieces.

- 1/4 cup peanuts.

- 1 tbsp. coconut oil.

For the salad:

- 1 cup green beans, (a large handful).

- 1 tbsp lime juice (juice of half a lime).

- 1 tsp sesame oil.

- 2 cups red cabbage, shredded.

- 1 carrot, shredded or grated.

For the rice:

- 1 cup red rice, or brown.

- A handful of basil leaves, or fresh herbs of your choice.

Directions:

For the tomato sambal:

1. Starting with 2 chili put all active ingredients into a blender and procedure until reasonably smooth. Taste and include more chilies up until the sambal is at your desired level of spiciness. Adjust flavoring to taste, with more salt or sugar.

For the rice:

2. Prepare rice according to packet directions.

For the salad:

3. While your rice is cooking, prepare your salad.
4. Bring water to a boil in a little pan. Blanch green beans for three minutes, then get rid of a colander/sieve and run under cold water to cool right away.
5. Put shredded red cabbage, carrot and beans into a blending bowl.
6. Put over the lime juice and sesame oil and toss to coat.

To serve:

7. Serve Bali bowls with a portion of red rice and
    salad, leading with the hot tempeh and
    peanuts, a handful of fresh herbs, and extra
    tomato sambal on the side.

Vegan Breakfast Muffins

Ingredients:

- 1 teaspoon coconut powder

- 250ml sweetened soy milk

- 1 apple, peeled and grated

- 2 tbsp grape seed oil

- 3 tablespoons nut butter (we utilized almond)

- 4 tablespoons demerara sugar

- 150g muesli mixture

- 50g light brown soft sugar

- 160g plain flour

- 50g pecans, About chilled

Directions:

1. Heating the oven to 200C/180C fan/gas 6. Line a muffin tin with instances.

2. Mix 100g muesli with the light brown sugar, flour and baking powder in a bowl.

3. Blend the milk, oil, apple and 2 tablespoons nut butter in a jug, then stir into the dry mix.

4. Divide both between the circumstances. Mix the remaining muesli with the sugar remaining nut butter along with the pecans, and spoon over the cakes.

5. Bake for 25-30 mins or until the cakes are golden and rose. Will keep for 3 to three days in an airtight container or suspend for a single month. Refresh from the oven prior to serving.

Cinnamon & Blueberry French Toast

Ingredients:

- 200ml oat milk or milk milk

- 1 tablespoon golden caster sugar

- 1 teaspoon vanilla extract

- 6 pieces of thick white bread

- Jojoba oil, for a frying pan

- 3 tablespoons walnut syrup

- 150g blueberries

- 2 tbsp gram flour

- 2 tbsp ground almonds

- 2 tsp cinnamon

- Icing sugar for dusting

DIRECTIONS:

1. Gradually Warmth the maple syrup and blueberries in a saucepan until the berries begin to pop up and release their juices, and then place them to a side in the pan. Whisk the flour, almonds, cinnamon, vanilla, and milk together in a shallow bowl.

2. Heating Just a little oil in a skillet. Dip a piece of bread into the milk mixture, shake off any excess, and fry the bread on both sides until it browns and crisps in the borders.

3. Keep the pieces warm in a very low oven since you cook the rest of the Serve with all the blueberries spo2d over and dust with icing sugar.

Tomato Basil Soup

Ingredients:

- 3 cups of fresh tomato puree (you can add fresh tomato stem)

- Salted butter stick

- 6 ounces cream cheese

- 1 handful fresh basil leaves

- Black pepper and salt to taste.

Directions:

1. Reduce enough fresh tomatoes to pulp in a blender that adds up to 4 cups of tomato puree.

2. Transfer puree to a large pot and add in cream cheese and salted butter.

3. Allow to heat and simmer, cook until cream cheese and butter melt.

4. Carefully pour the soup into the food processor, add fresh basil leaves and mix until smooth.

Cold Avocado Mint Soup

Ingredients:

- ½ cup cold coconut milk

- 1 ripe avocado

- L teaspoon lemon juice

- 1 romaine lettuce leaves

- 10 fresh mint leaves

- Salt to taste

Directions:

1. Add all ingredients in a food processor, and mix until smooth. The thickness of the soup should not be as thick as puree.

2. Pour the ingredients in the soup bowl and keep in the fridge for 4-8 minutes and serve.

Cheese Broccoli Soup

Ingredients:

- 2 cloves garlic, minced

- 2 cups chicken broth, or vegetable broth

- 2 cups cheddar cheese, chopped

- 2 cups broccoli, cut into flowers

- Cream cup heavy cream.

Directions:

1. In a medium high heat, in a large saucepan, add a little oil and pan-fry minced garlic.

2. Add vegetable broth or chicken broth, broccoli florets, heavy cream and increase heat to high.

3. Bring to the boil and turn down the heat, broccoli is cooked and leave to simmer for 10-15 minutes until tender.

4. Gently place the sliced cheddar cheese and stir occasionally. Stir until the cheese melts.

5. And keep shaking another batch of Cheddar cheese until all the sliced cheese has completely melted, doing so until you get the cheese out.

6. Once all the cheese has melted, turn it off completely. Make sure to reduce heat and reduce boil, making sure the heat is not kept on high to avoid confiscation.

Peach Pancakes

Ingredients:

- Tapioca, 1/4 cup

- Coconut oil, melted, 2 tablespoon

- Cassava flour, 1/4cup

- Seasalt, 1 teaspoon

- Baking soda, ¼ teaspoon

- Baking powder, 1/2 teaspoon

- 2 peaches, ripe. Peeled and sliced into thin slices

- Vanilla extract, 1 teaspoon

- 2 large eggs

- Monk fruit or stevia, 1 teaspoon

- Kefir or coconut yogurt, 5 ounces

- Coconut flour, ¼ cup

- Cinnamon sprinkled over the peaches

Directions:

1. Prepare the oven by preheating to a temperature of 350 degrees and prepare a pie tray or pan with butter.
2. Using a lg bowl, add eggs, sweetener, kefir or coconut yogurt, and vanilla extract.
3. When adding these items into the bowl, gradually pour the coconut oil and whisk it continuously, to avoid the oil from sticking or becoming solid.
4. This is especially a concern if the room temperature is a bit cooler than usual.
5. Combine the cassava flour, coconut flour, sea salt, tapioca flour, baking soda, and baking powder, using a med bowl, and blend well,

then gently combine with the wet ingredients, a little at a time, until a smooth batter is formed.

6. Pour the batter into a pie pan and place the peach slices on top of the batter, then sprinkle with cinnamon evenly.

7. Cinnamon can also be sprinkled or coated over the peaches while mixing ingredients.

8. Cook for 30 min, then test with a toothpick to ensure it comes out clean, which means the pie-pancake is ready.

9. Serve with additional peach slices and whipped cream (coconut or dairy), and cinnamon.

Egg And Arugula

Ingredients:

- Balsamic vinegar, 2 tablespoons

- Sea salt, 1/2 teaspoon

- 3 eggs

- Olive oil, 3 tablespoons, divided

- Fresh Arugula, 2 cups (chopped)

Directions:

1. Using med heat and a lg skillet warm olive oil.
2. Using a sm bowl, whisk the balsamic vinegar, and sea salt together until well combined.
3. In a second bowl, whisk the eggs and add any desired spices, such as black pepper, paprika, etc. until blended.

4. Pour the eggs to scramble in the skillet, mixing
    evenly until they are well cooked.

5. Remove to a medium bowl, then mix the
    chopped arugula and drizzle the dressing over
    the dish to serve

Arugula Chicken Salad With Lemon Vinaigrette

Ingredients:

Chicken

- 1 tablespoon avocado oil

- 4 ounces of skinless, b2less chicken breast, cut into equal strips

- 1 tablespoon of lemon juice

- 1/4 teaspoon of iodized sea salt

- Zest of 1/2 lemon (optional)

Dressing

- 2 tablespoons extra-virgin olive oil

- 2 tablespoons of lemon juice

- 1/2 diced avocado

- Sea salt to taste

Salad

- 1 1/2 cups chopped arugula

- Pan fried mushrooms

Directions:

1. Heat the avocado oil in a small pan on high heat.
2. Place the chicken strips in the pan and pour the lemon juice and salt. Fry the chicken strips for 2 minutes; turn them and fry for another 2 minutes, until they're completely cooked.
3. Remove and save.
4. For the dressing, put 1 tablespoon of lemon juice over the avocado, and the bind the other lemon juice tablespoon with the olive oil and salt in a jar and shake until is homogeneous.
5. Add to the arugula and mushrooms.

6. Top with the chicken and pour some lemon
    zest.

93

Chicken Nori Wrap With Cilantro Dip

Ingredients:

Chicken nori wrap

- 4 ounces of skinless, b2less chicken breast, cut into equal strips

- 1 tablespoon of lemon juice

- 1 cup of arugula

- 1 sheet of nori

- 1/4 teaspoon of iodized sea salt

- 1 tablespoon avocado oil

- 4 green olives in halves

Cilantro dip

- 1/4 cup extra-virgin olive oil

- Iodized sea salt to taste

- 2 cups of diced cilantro

- 2 tablespoons of lemon juice

Directions:

1. Heat the avocado oil in a small pan on high heat.
2. Place the chicken strips in the pan and pour 1 tablespoon lemon juice and salt.
3. Fry the chicken strips for 2 minutes; turn them and fry for another 2 minutes, until they're completely cooked.
4. Remove and save.
5. Pour the avocado into the other lemon juice tablespoon and add salt.
6. For the dip, just add all the ingredients into a blender and process them.
7. To serve, put the arugula in the bottom half of the nori sheet.

8. Top it with the chicken, lemon-avocado and optionally, olives.

9. Add a little salt if you like.

10. Roll it helping yourself with the bamboo mat if you like and seal the end with a drop of water.

11. Cut it in halves to serve it with the dip.

Food Scramble

Ingredients:

- 1 teaspoon garlic powder

- 2 cups kale, fresh, trimmed and chopped

- 2 tablespoons olive oil

- 4 fresh organic eggs

- Black pepper and salt to taste

Directions:

1. In a mixing bowl, add eggs and beat well. Set aside.
2. In a skillet, heat the oil over medium heat and cook the kale for 2 minutes.
3. Add eggs and remaining ingredients and cook for 4 minutes stirring often.
4. Serve hot and enjoy!

Sweet Omelet

Ingredients:

- ¼ teaspoon ground cinnamon

- ½ large green apple, cored and thinly sliced

- 2 teaspoons olive oil, divided

- Pinch of salt

- 1/8 teaspoon organic vanilla extract

- 2 large organic eggs

- ¼ teaspoon nutmeg

Directions:

1. In a non-stick frying pan, heat the 1 teaspoon of oil over medium-low heat and cook apple slices, nutmeg, and cinnamon for about 5

minutes, turning once halfway through the cook time.

2. In a mixing bowl, add eggs, vanilla and salt beat until fluffy.

3. Add remaining oil into the pan and allow it to melt completely.

4. Add the egg mixture over apple slices evenly, cook for 4 minutes.

5. Carefully, turn the pan over a serving plate and then fold the omelet and serve hot.

Mixed Vegetable Sichuan

Ingredients:

- 1 2/3 cups of carrots sliced into very thin strips

- 1 red bell pepper, deseeded and sliced into very thin strips

- 2 cups shiitake mushrooms sliced (you can use other mushrooms if you can't find shiitake).

- 2 cups mange tout (snow peas)

- 3 tablespoons of soy sauce

- 3 tablespoons crunchy peanut butter

- 4 cups bean sprouts

- 2 tablespoons sesame oil

- 4 garlic cloves, crushed

- A large thumb size piece of fresh ginger, peeled and grated

- 2 cups rice, cooked washed in cold water and drained

Directions:

1. Heat the sesame oil in a preheated wok or deep skillet and fry the ginger and carrots for 2 minutes. Add the red pepper and garlic and stir-fry for another 2 minutes. Then add the mushrooms and mange tout and stir-fry for a further minute.

2. In a small bowl, combine the soy sauce and peanut butter until mixed thoroughly.

3. Put on a kettle of water to boil.

4. Make a space in the center of the stir-fried vegetables with a wooden spoon so that the base of the wok is visible. Pour in the sauce and bring to the boil, stirring continually until it starts to thicken. Finally, add the

beansprouts and toss them through the
vegetables to coat thoroughly with the sauce.

5. Pour the kettle of boiling water through the
    pre-cooked rice and drain.

6. Plate up the rice into individual bowls and
    place the stir fry on top. Serve immediately.

Fresh Green Thai Curry

Ingredients:

Curry paste

- Rind and juice of 1 lime and 1 small lemon

- Large bunch of cilantros washed and chopped (including stalks)

- 2 tablespoons soy sauce

- 1 x 13.5 fluid oz can of organic unsweetened coconut milk (full fat)

- 4 stalks of lemon grass (outer peel removed before chopping finely)

- Good thumb size piece of fresh ginger peeled and grated

- 6 green chilies de-seeded and chopped

Curry

- 2 cups (packed) kale, chopped with stalk removed

- 10 fine fresh asparagus spears cut into 2-inch pieces

- 2 cups Thai rice

- Black pepper

- 2 cups of chick peas cooked and rinsed

- 2 cups green peas or snow peas

Garnish

- Some of the cilantro leaves reserved

- 1 lime cut into quarters

Directions:

1. To make the curry paste, add all the ingredients except the coconut milk and soy

sauce, to a blender or food processor and blend until they form a paste.

2. Add the coconut milk to the paste and blend again until fully combined.

3. Finally, add the soy sauce and mix it in.

4. Cook the rice following the manufacturer's guidelines, when it is cooked drain and rinse it thoroughly in cold water, drain again and set aside.

5. Meanwhile in a skillet put the chickpeas and curry sauce you have just made, season with some freshly ground black pepper and cook covered on a low heat for 15 minutes.

6. Add the kale and peas and cook covered for a further 5 minutes or until the kale has wilted.

7. While the curry is cooking, fry the asparagus gently until golden.

8. Boil a kettle full of water.

9. Add the asparagus to the curry remove from the heat and keep covered.

10. Pour the boiling water all over the rice, allowing the water to drain, then immediately plate it up.

11. Put the curry on top of the rice and sprinkle a little of the reserved cilantro on top to garnish.

12. Add a wedge of lime to the plate and serve immediately.

13. You can prepare the curry paste including the coconut milk and soy sauce ahead of time and refrigerate it in an airtight container for up to 5 days or freeze for up to 2 months.

Thai Coconut Curry Bowl

Ingredients:

- ½ cup sliced zucchini

- ¼ cup sliced red onion

- 2 tablespoons Thai red curry paste

- 1 can (13.5 oz) coconut milk

- 1 cup cooked brown rice or rice noodles

- ½ cup tofu or tempeh, cubed and stir-fried ½ cup sliced bell peppers

- Fresh cilantro and lime wedges for garnish

Directions:

1. In a large skillet, sauté the bell peppers, zucchini, and re domino until tender.

2. Stir in the Thai red curry paste and cook for another minute.

3. Pour in the coconut milk and simmer until heated through.

4. In a bowl, place the cooked brown rice or rice noodles, tofu or temper, and the curry mixture.

5. Garnish with fresh cilantro and serve with lime wedges for added flavor.

6. Enjoy this aromatic and satisfying Thai-inspired grain bowl.

7. Feel free to explore different flavor profiles, ingredients, and dressings to suit your preferences and create your unique grain bowls.

8. These hearty grain bowls are versatile, filling, and can be enjoyed as a complete meal packed with wholesome goodness.

9. Get creative and enjoy the delicious
    combinations and nourishing benefits they
    offer!

Blueberry Muffins

Ingredients:

- ½ teaspoon baking soda

- ¼ teaspoon salt

- 1 cup plant-based milk (such as almond or oat milk) ½ cup unsweetened applesauce

- ¼ cup melted coconut oil or vegetable oil 1 teaspoon vanilla extract

- 2 cups all-purpose flour

- ½ cup granulated sugar

- 2 teaspoons baking powder

- 1 cup fresh or frozen blueberries

Directions:

1. Preheat the oven to 375°F (190°C) and line a muffin tin with paper liners.
2. In a large mixing bowl, combine the flour, sugar, baking powder, baking soda, and salt.
3. In a separate bowl, whisk together the plant-based milk,
4. applesauce, melted coconut oil, and vanilla extract.
5. Pour the wet ingredients into the dry ingredients and stir until just combined.
6. Gently fold in the blueberries.
7. Divide the batter evenly among the muffin cups, filling them about three-quarters full.
8. Bake for 18-20 minutes or until a toothpick inserted into the center comes out clean.
9. Allow the muffins to cool in the tin for a few minutes before transferring them to a wire rack to cool completely.
10. Enjoy these moist and fruity blueberry muffins as a delightful snack or breakfast treat.

Sorghum Salad With Radicchio

Ingredients:

Baslc SORGHUM

- 1 tablespoon extra-virgin olive oil

- 1 teaspoon ocean salt, ideally iodized

- 1 cup sorghum

- 3 cups vegetable stock or water, in addition to more if essential

Dressing

- Serving of mixed greens

- 1/2 cup cleaved pecans or walnuts

- 1 head radicchio, torn or cleaved into scaled down pieces

- 1/2 cup cleaved level leaf parsley

- 3 tablespoons balsamic vinegar or other vinegar

- 4 tablespoons extra-virgin olive oil

- 3 tablespoons escapades, washed

- 1 teaspoon coriander powder or seeds

- 1 clove garlic, stripped

Directions:

1. Make the sorghum. Pick through the sorghum, flush, and dispose of any flotsam and jetsam.

2. Put the stock or water and oil in a medium pan, and heat to the point of boiling. Mix in the sorghum and come back to a bubble.

3. Diminish the warmth to a stew, spread, and cook for 1 to 2 hours, blending at regular intervals and including stock or water as expected to shield it from drying out or adhering to the skillet.

4. To test for d2ness, mix with a fork: the sorghum is d2 when it is light and fluffy.

5. You can make the formula early as yet. Refrigerate or stop the cooked sorghum, and afterward defrost and give it a chance to come to room temperature when you need to utilize it.

6. Then again, finish the dish promptly if you intend to serve while the sorghum is warm.

7. Make the dressing. Utilizing a magic bullet blender or a scaled down nourishment processor fitted with a s-sharp edge, consolidate the vinegar, olive oil, escapades, coriander, and garlic and procedure until smooth.

8. To serve. Blend the readied sorghum, nuts, radicchio, and parsley in a huge bowl. Add the dressing and hurl to consolidate. Serve on supper plates.

Moroccan Spiced Chicken With Millet Tubule

Ingredients:

For the chicken

- 1/2 teaspoon cumin

- 1/2 teaspoon paprika

- 1/2 teaspoon dark pepper

- 1/2 teaspoon Turmeric

- 1/2 teaspoon iodized ocean salt

- 4 field raised chicken thighs

- 2 cups coconut yogurt, plain

- Juice of 2 lemon

- Get-up-and-go of lemon

- Get-up-and-go of 2 orange

- 1/2 teaspoon cinnamon

For the tubule

- 1 teaspoon iodized ocean salt

- 1 tablespoon additional virgin the entirety of oil

- Juice of 2 lemon

- 2 cups cooked millet

- 1/2 cup minced parsley

- 1/2 cup minced implied

- 1/4 cup minced dill

- 1/4 cup red wine vinegar

Directions:

1. Marinate the chicken: in a huge Ziploc sack, join the yogurt, lemon juice, lemon pizzazz,

orange get-up-and-go, and flavors. Include the chicken, and marinate for in any event 60 minutes. (If utilizing transitory, utilize a similar marinade, however for 30 minutes.)

2. Preheat the stove to 375°F, set up an oven container or a sheet plate with wire rack by spring with oil. Put in a safe spot.

3. Make the tubule: join all fixings in an enormous bowl, and mix well. Give the flavors a chance to merge for at any rate 20 minutes (which is immaculate, since you need that opportunity to cook the chicken).

4. Expel chicken of bread and brackets or tempeh) for marinade, pat dry with paper towels, and the range on the readied preparing sheet. If your chicken has skin, place it's going down.

5. Prepare the chicken for 20 to 25 minutes, then flip and heat for an extra 10 to 15

minutes, skin side up, and disclose to me it has come to

6. 165°F and skin is fresh. Expel from warmth, and left rest five minutes before serving.

7. If utilizing tempeh: heat for 12 to 15 minutes, flipping once in a while, until firm. Expel from warmth and serve right away.

8. To make it veggie lover, use about a pound of tempeh, cut into thick cuts.

Cabbage-Kale Sauté With Salmon And Avocado

Ingredients:

- 4 pinches sea salt, preferably iodized

- 3 tablespoons avocado oil

- 1½ cups finely sliced green cabbage

- ½ red onion, thinly sliced

- ½ avocado, diced

- 3 tablespoons freshly squeezed lemon juice

- 3 ounces wild-caught Alaska salmon

Directions:

1. Toss the diced avocado in 1 tablespoon of the lemon juice and season with a pinch of salt. Set aside.

2. Heat a skillet over medium heat. When it is hot, add 2 tablespoons of the avocado oil and

the cabbage and onion. Sauté until tender, about 10 minutes, stirring occasionally. Season with 2 more pinches of salt. Using a slotted spatula, remove from the skillet and set aside.

3. Add the remaining 1 tablespoon avocado oil to the skillet, raise the heat to high, and add the remaining 2 tablespoons lemon juice and the salmon. Sear the salmon, flipping after 3 minutes, until cooked through, about 6 minutes total. Season with the remaining pinch salt.

4. To serve, top the sautéed cabbage and onions with the salmon and avocado.

Roasted Broccoli With Cauliflower "Rice" And Sautéed Onions

Ingredients:

CAULIFLOWER "RICE"

- 1 tablespoon avocado oil

- 1 tablespoon freshly squeezed lemon juice

- ¼ teaspoon curry powder

- ½ head medium cauliflower, riced (see headnote)

- 1 pinch sea salt, preferably iodized

Broccoli

- 1½ cups cut-up broccoli florets

- 1½ tablespoons avocado oil

- 1 pinch sea salt, preferably iodized

Curried onions

- ½ red onion, thinly sliced

- ½ tablespoon avocado oil

- Pinch sea salt, preferably iodized

Directions:

1. Heat the oven to 375°F, Sauté the cauliflower in a medium skillet with 1 tablespoon of the avocado oil, the lemon juice, curry powder, and a pinch of salt until tender, 3 to 5 minutes.

2. Do not let it get mushy by overcooking. Transfer the cauliflower "rice" to a plate and keep warm. Wipe the skillet clean with a paper towel.

3. Put the broccoli in a Pyrex dish with 1 tablespoon of the avocado oil. Roast in the oven for 15 minutes, stirring twice, until tender. Season with a pinch of salt.

4. Reheat the skillet over medium heat. When it
    is hot, add the remaining ½ tablespoon
    avocado oil and the sliced onion and sauté
    until tender, stirring frequently, for about 5
    minutes. Season with a pinch of salt.
5. To serve, place the cauliflower "rice" on a
    plate and top with the broccoli and sautéed
    onions.

Cornmeal And Blueberry Pancakes

Ingredients:

- 2 tsp. baking powder

- 2-third tsp. baking soda

- 2-5th tsp. of salt

- 2 cup of blueberries

- 2 cup of soy milk

- Half cup of each

- Water

- Cornmeal (ground)

- 2 and a half cup of wheat flour

- 3 tbsps. of vegetable oil

Directions:

1. Preheat your oven at 95 degrees Celsius.

2. Combine water and soy milk in a bowl.

3. Take a large mixing bowl and combine cornmeal, baking soda, flour, salt, and baking powder.

4. Add the mixture of soy milk. Combine properly. Add the blueberries and allow the batter to rest for five minutes.

5. Take a large skillet and grease it using oil. Add 2-5th cup of the batter in the skillet.

6. Cook until the pancakes are bubbly on the top, and the edges are dry. Cook for five minutes on each side. Repeat with the remaining batter.

7. Serve hot with jam or syrup.

Breakfast Tortilla

Ingredients:

- 4 large eggs (beaten)

- 2 tbsp. of mayonnaise

- 5 tortillas (flour)

- 3 tbsps. of beans (refried)

- 4 tbsps. of salsa

- 2 and a half cup of lettuce (shredded)

Directions:

1. Combine salsa and beans in a small bowl.
2. Take an iron skillet and heat oil in it. Add the eggs and let the bottom set—Cook for 2 minute.

3. Spread the mixture of beans on half of the egg and flip 2 side for making the shape of a half-circle. Cook until the eggs set properly.

4. Spread mayonnaise on the tortillas.

5. Cut the cooked eggs into 5 equal pieces. Place each piece of eggs on the tortillas. Top with lettuce.

6. Roll the tortillas. Serve hot.

Macaroons

Ingredients:

- 1 teaspoon of vanilla or almond extract

- 3 cups of raw oats

- 2 tablespoons maple syrup

- 1/3 cup of coconut oil

- 1 cup of shredded coconut

- 5 tablespoons of cocoa powder

- ½ cups of coconut milk

Directions:

1. Combine the coconut milk, oil, vanilla or almond extract, and maple syrup into a bowl and stir together.

2. In a different container, combine the cocoa

powder, shredded coconut, and raw oats.

3. Combine both bowls of ingredients and form

into balls. Refrigerate for at least 3 hours

before servings.

Kale Chips

131

Ingredients:

- 1 tablespoon of sea salt

- 1 bunch of kale

- 2 tablespoons of olive oil

Directions:

1. Wash and drain 2 bunch of kale, then remove stems and slice into 2 or 3-inch pieces (chip or bite-sized). Lightly coat each kale piece in olive oil, and place on a large, lined baking sheet.
2. Sprinkle each kale slice with sea salt and preheat the oven, setting to 350 degrees.
3. Bake for 8-10 minutes or until crispy, but not burnt.

Fruit And Nut Oatmeal

Ingredients:

- ½ ripe banana, sliced (optional)

- 2 tablespoons of chopped nuts, such as walnuts, pecans, or cashews

- (optional)

- 2 tablespoons of dried fruit, such as raisins, cranberries, chopped apples, chopped

- Apricots (optional)

- ¾ cup of rolled oats

- ¼ teaspoon ground cinnamon

- Pinch of sea salt

- ¼ cup fresh berries (optional)

- Maple syrup (optional)

Directions:

1. Cook oats in water in a saucepan until it starts boiling. Reduce the heat and let it simmer for about 5 minutes.
2. Add cinnamon and salt – stirring. Top with berries and fruits and serve while hot.

Red Pesto And Kale Porridge

Ingredients:

- 1 cup of chopped kale

- 1 cup of sliced cherry tomatoes

- 1 scallion

- 1 teaspoon of tahini

- 1 tablespoon of pesto of your choice

- 2 tablespoons of nutritional yeast

- 1 tablespoon of pumpkin seed

- 1 tablespoon of hemp seed

- ½ cup of oats

- ½ cup of couscous

- 2 cups of veggie stock (or water)

- 1 teaspoon of dried oregano

- 1 teaspoon of dried basil

- Salt and pepper to taste

Directions:

1. Cook oats, couscous, vegetable stock, oregano, basil, salt and pepper in a small pot on medium heat for about 5 minutes stirring occasionally.

2. Once it becomes creamy, add scallions, chopped kale, and tomatoes. Stir in pesto, yeast, and tahini.

3. Top with some cherry tomatoes hemp seeds and pumpkin and serve it warm.

Spicy Tofu Scramble

Ingredients:

- 1 avocado, sliced

- 1 teaspoon of ground turmeric

- 2 teaspoon of ground black salt

- Salt & pepper to taste

- 1 to 2 tablespoons of olive oil

- 350g of firm tofu

- 2 small spring onions, sliced

- 1 large garlic clove, finely chopped

- 10 cherry tomatoes, halved

- ½ fresh red chili, sliced

- 8 slices of gluten-free bread, toasted

Directions:

1. Sauté garlic in olive oil in a pan.

2. Add in tomatoes and cook until they're soft then remove the mixture from the pan.

3. Under a grill, toast bread slices. Sauté some onions and chili seeds on low-medium heat until they soften and add tofu.

4. Sprinkle with turmeric and black salt and stir it for a couple of minutes. Finally, add tomatoes and garlic back to the pan to warm up.

5. Add the tofu scramble onto the toasted bread slices and decorate with avocado. Season as desired. Enjoy!

Scrambled Tofu Breakfast Burrito

Ingredients:

Tofu:

- 1/2 tsp chili powder.

- 1/2 tsp cumin.

- 1 tsp dietary yeast.

- 1/4 tsp sea salt.

- 1 pinch cayenne pepper .

- 1 12-ounce bundle firm or extra-firm tofu.

- 1 tsp oil (or 1 tbsp (15 ml) water).

- 3 cloves garlic (minced).

- 1 tbsp hummus (store-bought or DIY).

- 1/4 cup minced parsley.

Vegetables:

- 1/2 tsp ground cumin.

- 1/2 tsp chili powder (not ground chili).

- 2 cups chopped kale.

- 5 whole baby potatoes.

- 1 medium red bell pepper.

- 1 tsp oil.

- 1 pinch sea salt.

The rest:

- 3-4 large flour or gluten-free tortillas (ensure vegan-friendly - I like TJ's brand).

- 1 medium ripe avocado (chopped or mashed).

- Cilantro.

- Chunky green or red salsa or hot sauce.

Directions:

1. Preheat oven to 400° F (204° C) and line a baking sheet with parchment paper (use more baking sheets if increasing batch size).

2. In the meantime, likewise, wrap tofu in a clean towel and set something heavy on top - such as a cast-iron skillet - to push out excess wetness.

3. fall apart with a fork into fine pieces. Set aside.

4. Add potatoes and red pepper to the baking sheet, drizzle with oil (or water) and spices, and toss to combine. Bake for 15-22 minutes or until fork-tender and a little browned. Include kale in the last 5 minutes of baking to wilt, tossing with the other veggies to integrate seasonings.

5. In the meantime, heat a large skillet over medium heat.

6. As soon as hot, include oil (or water), garlic, and tofu and sauté for 7-10 minutes, stirring often, to slightly brown.

7. In the meantime, to a small blending bowl, include the hummus, chili powder, cumin, nutritional yeast, salt, and cayenne (optional). Continue adding water until the formation of a pourable sauce.

8. Add the spice mix to the tofu and continue cooking over medium heat up until slightly browned - 3-5 minutes.

9. Include generous portions of the roasted vegetables, scrambled tofu, avocado, cilantro, and a bit of salsa.

10. Continue until all garnishes are used up - about 3-4 large burritos.

11. Delight in instantly for most excellent outcomes. Alternatively, you can package and refrigerate these up to 4 days (or the freezer for 1 month). If heating in microwave, simply

microwave or heat in the oven before eating

(be sure to eliminate foil).